IMAGES OF THE
SUFFOLK COAST

Photographed by John Curtis

SALMON

INTRODUCTION

The unspoilt and beautiful Suffolk coastline has for well over a century been a popular destination with its old fishing villages, beaches, crumbling cliffs, open heathland, salt marshes and river estuaries. It somehow retains an atmosphere redolent of an earlier age as if it has been bypassed by the busy modern world. There are several long estuaries along this coast which ensure that the major roads pass well inland, and so the coast preserves a special sense of tranquillity.

Dotted with villages and towns which date back to before the Domesday Book, the true beauty is perhaps best revealed while taking a walk along the Suffolk Coast and Heaths Path, which follows this ever-changing and remote coastline.

Stretching for some fifty miles from the village of Kessingland, in the north, to the Stour estuary, near Felixstowe in the south, the Suffolk Heritage Coast is under constant attack from the sea which has swallowed entire villages that now lie beneath the waves.

The quiet little village of Dunwich was once one of the leading ports on the east coast, but the sea claimed much of the town and took six churches, a monastery, and three chapels. Legend has it that the church bells can still be heard ringing below the waves.

The coast is also famous for its quality of light and wide open skies which have inspired many artists and writers over the years, such as Arthur Ransome, Benjamin Britten and Charles Rennie Mackintosh.

The history of this region is a long and fascinating one. After the end of the Roman occupation, Suffolk was settled by the Angles in the 5th century and became part of the

Martello Tower on Aldeburgh Beach

Kingdom of East Anglia, as evidenced by the famous Anglo-Saxon burial site of Sutton Hoo, near Woodbridge. It also is from this time the name 'Suffolk' originates, as it described the southern half of the kingdom, the 'South Folk'.

During the Middle Ages, as the county became a major player in the wool trade, Suffolk's coastal towns gained in importance as they started trading up and down the east coast and across the North Sea. Later, with the coming of the railway in the 1850s and industrialisation, the coast was finally connected to Ipswich and beyond, giving rise to the growth of elegant small resorts like Southwold and Aldeburgh. At the same time, the population grew rapidly thereby changing both the economic status and physical appearance of Suffolk.

The historic importance of Suffolk is also reflected in the numbers of large churches, particularly in the area around Southwold, which now seem out of proportion to the size of the villages they serve. At Blythburgh, Holy Trinity Church dominates the countryside, living up to its name of the "Cathedral of the Marshes", while at Walberswick and Covehithe, the ruins of much grander churches now stand enveloping smaller parish churches.

The Suffolk coast and the beautiful heaths which lie behind have been designated an Area of Outstanding Natural Beauty for over 40 years. It covers an area of 150 square miles and attracts large numbers of bird-watchers and other nature lovers. The superb wetlands and salt marshes, which fringe the coast, support some of the rarest wildlife in the country, and the rivers and estuaries teem with wading birds and wildfowl. Some of the best-loved nature reserves are at Minsmere and Dunwich Heath where avocet, bitterns, and marsh harriers can be seen in addition to numerous butterflies and wildflowers.

Dunwich Beach

Bawdsey

During the Second World War, the little hamlet of Bawdsey was home to the development of radar by Sir Robert Watson-Watt and his team. Further south on the peninsula, at the entrance to the River Deben estuary, is Bawdsey Quay where a small passenger ferry plies the waters of the river mouth to Felixstowe.

Felixstowe Ferry

A few miles north-east of the pleasant family resort of Felixstowe, is the hamlet of Felixstowe Ferry where the boat house of the local sailing club dominates the little quay. Inland, the gently undulating landscape lends itself well to a large golf course, while along the coastline, the Martello Towers still stand guard on the beach.

Tide Mill, Woodbridge

Until the silting up of the river, Woodbridge was a major shipbuilding centre providing warships for the Royal Navy. Today it is a lively sailing centre used by pleasure craft and has a modern marina and excellent moorings at the Tidemill Yacht Harbour. Overlooking the river estuary is the picturesque white weather-boarded Tide Mill which was built in the 1790s. The successor to a series of mills which have stood here since 1170, the mill has been beautifully restored and put back to full working order.

Shire Hall, Woodbridge

The beautiful ancient market town of Woodbridge, situated on the River Deben, is one of Suffolk's many fine gems. On Market Hill, in the centre of the town, stands the Shire Hall which dates from Elizabethan times. Recently restored, it was originally financed by Thomas Seckford, who was a benefactor of the town. The handsome hall has served many different purposes over the years.

Ye Olde Bell & Steelyard, Woodbridge

Set in the centre of historic Woodbridge in New Street, Ye Olde Bell & Steelyard dates back to the 16th century. Hanging off the front of the building is the 'steelyard', a device constructed to weigh carts and loads in the days before the public weighbridge. The interior of the pub features massive oak beams and three fireplaces.

River Deben at Woodbridge

As the River Deben winds its way through the eastern part of Suffolk, mudflats are created which provide the local wildlife with invaluable habitats. Near Woodbridge, this flock of Canada geese have come to rest by the banks of the river. Towards the sea, the entrance to the river is also known for its fine bass fishing.

Sutton Hoo

Across the river from Woodbridge is Sutton Hoo, a large Anglo-Saxon burial site of major importance, where the ship burial of one of the earliest English kings was found and excavated in 1939. Now in the care of The National Trust, a full-size reconstruction of the burial chamber can be seen here, along with many original finds and replicas. The beautiful 255-acre estate also offers lovely walks and far-reaching views of the River Deben estuary.

All Saints' Church, Ramsholt

Standing in isolation inland from the quay, at Ramsholt, is All Saints, one of Suffolk's many delightful round tower churches. The church dates back to the Normans with some later medieval additions. After becoming derelict, it was lovingly restored in the 1850s when the porch was added, and it is still in use today. The unusual buttressing on the tower makes it appear oval from a distance as it stands proudly looking out over the river.

River Deben at Ramsholt

Although the river is tidal, it offers prime sailing for both novices and the more experienced sailor. In summer, yachts and smaller pleasure boats throng here taking advantage of the many excellent moorings. Ramsholt was once the first landing on the north shore of the river after Bawdsey and was a flourishing village.

Ramsholt Quay

Nestling in a little bend in the River Deben, is Ramsholt Quay, a popular stopping point centred round a sandy beach and the popular Ramsholt Arms pub. The tiny beach attracts both local residents and visitors, and the quayside, once busy with barges and other cargo boats, is now visited by pleasure craft of all kinds.

Orford Haven

The Rivers Ore and Alde estuaries reach the sea at Orford Haven. It lies behind the tip of a narrow shingle spit which continues northwards past Orford to Aldeburgh. The tidal mudflats here provide a fine habitat for many species of birds, including cormorants, herons, avocets, oyster catchers and curlews.

Shingle Street

A single row of assorted holiday homes make up this once thriving fishing village, set just behind the shifting banks of shingle, at the mouth of Orford Ness. The first cottages here were built in the early 1800s at the same time as the Martello Towers that dot the coastline. Many fascinating legends are also attached to this remote place.

Rendlesham Forest

East of Woodbridge lies Rendlesham Forest, part of the coastal heathland belt, known as the Sandlings. A lovely site for picnics and walks, there are several well-laid out trails, one of which commemorates the great storm of 1987, and one which relates to the UFO sightings of 1980.

Butley Priory

The magnificent gatehouse is all that remains of Butley Priory, which was founded here in 1171 by Augustinian monks. The original collection of buildings covered almost 20 acres and were enclosed by a stone wall. An extensive armorial frieze adorns the north side and the beautiful stone used is thought to have come from the Valley of the Yonne, in France.

Orford Quay

Orford was once a busy medieval riverside port which traded in fish and wool. The delightful quay is still a focal point with little fish stalls lining the river bank. From here, a small passenger ferry provides the only access to Orford Ness across the River Ore. Orford is now cut off from the open sea by a six-mile-long spit of land, but boats can still be launched into the River Alde from the foreshore.

Orford Castle

The distinctive keep of Orford Castle and the tower of nearby St. Bartholomew's Church have provided shipping with landmarks since the 12th century. The castle was built by King Henry II as part of a network of coastal defences, and its unique polygonal tower keep remains remarkbly intact and still offers fine views over the town. The surrounding mounds and earthworks give a good idea of the size of the original structure.

Orford Ness

Orford Ness is the largest vegetated shingle spit in Europe. Wild and remote, and constantly changing, the ten-mile-long bank is today a renowned nature reserve, while decaying military structures highlight its world-affecting importance as the site of experiments in radar, bombs and atomic weapons. The Ness is also a significant breeding area for the rare little tern.

Orford Lighthouse

The red-banded Orford Ness Lighthouse stands out prominently across the shingle bank warning shipping away from the dangerous tides, offshore banks and shoals. Originally built for Lord Braybrooke of Audley End, the lighthouse is over 200 years old and has weathered both violent storms and times of war.

River Alde at Iken

The River Alde estuary at Iken, pronounced *eye-can*, is a haven for wildfowl and wading birds, with golden reeds and mudflats providing the perfect habitat. The cries of avocet and curlew ring across the reed beds and water at this isolated and beautiful place, which is now also home to several old Thames sailing barges. Dedicated to St. Botolph, Iken church was built on the highest point of a former island and stands in a prominent position looking out over the river.

Tunstall Forest

Another delightful woodland in the Sandlings area is Tunstall Forest, which is situated just south of Snape Maltings. Designated as a Site of Special Scientific Interest, the wood is popular with walkers, cyclists and horseriders alike, and an important part of the Suffolk Coast and Heaths Area of Outstanding Natural Beauty. Amongst the varied wildlife, which can be seen here, are fallow deer and muntjac.

Snape
These magnificent buildings just outside the village of Snape are home to the internationally renowned Aldeburgh Festival, which was founded in 1948, largely through the efforts of the composer, Benjamin Britten, and the singer, Peter Pears. Originally a 19th century malt house situated on the banks of the River Alde, the concert hall opened in 1967 and is surrounded by a complex which today covers some seven acres and includes shops, galleries, a bar and a restaurant. Devoted mainly to classical music, the festival also includes literature and poetry, drama, lectures and exhibitions of art.

Snape Maltings

Built on the banks of the River Alde in the 19th century by Newson Garrett, Snape Maltings continued to produce malt for the brewing of beer up until 1965. It was the largest barley maltings in East Anglia and the distinctive building was created especially for the sprouting and drying of barley to create barley malt.

Snape War Memorial

A memorial dedicated to the fallen of the Second World War stands in the churchyard of St. John the Baptist. The church is one mile from the village and houses a fine 15th century font. The east window was designed and made by Mary Lowndes in 1920, and depicts Snape Bridge as it once was along with an old Thames barge.

ERECTED IN HONOUR OF THE FALLEN

AIREY A.J.	GOODING S.	NEWSON B.
BATES C.R.	HAILL W.R.	OLDING F.C.
BERRY W.C.R.	HOWELL G.E.	PITHER C.K.
BONE F.	HOWELL W.G.	PITHER S.
COWELL C.E.M.	HUDSON H.	READ W.C.
CRANE H.H.	KING J.	READ W.G.
CURTIS A.C.	LAST H.J.	RIDGEON N.
DAVEY W.E.R.	LEE J.	SMITH A.
FOREMAN H.S.	LEEK F.W.	SMITH G.D.
GANT D.	MISS E.W.	SMITH

BARNES G.E. CHURCHILD K.C. JOHNSON S R.E. MASTER W.C. 1939–1945 PARKER H.W. SCARCE W.R. SMITH R. WELLS E.C.
HOWARD LOWE D. JO... B SMITH... THURKELL... D. WOODS C.H.

The Red House, Aldeburgh

This picturesque red-brick house was for many years the home of composer, Benjamin Britten, and tenor, Peter Pears, who both moved here in 1957. The house has its origins in the early 17th century when it started its life as a farmhouse. It was later bought by Thomas Wentworth, third Earl of Strafford, whose descendants eventually sold it on. During the 1950s, the artist and close friend of Britten, Mary Potter, lived here with her family. Today, it is the home of the Britten–Pears Foundation and holds a large archive collection.

The Scallop, Aldeburgh

Dedicated to composer Benjamin Britten, Maggi Hambling's evocative sculpture, *Scallop*, was unveiled in November 2003. The huge steel shell has a quote from Britten's opera *Peter Grimes* pierced along the top edge and is a symbol of the act of listening. This fascinating piece of art sits on the shingle just a short walk along the beach north of Aldeburgh.

Aldeburgh Beach

The small resort of Aldeburgh, with its one main street of elegant houses and narrow lanes flanked by quaint old cottages, was once an important east coast harbour. The now quiet coastal resort also had a flourishing shipbuilding industry where Sir Francis Drake's ship, *Golden Hind*, was built. Aldeburgh still retains a small fishing fleet of colourful fishing boats which are launched directly off the shelved shingle beach. The freshly caught fish and seafood are sold from the little fishermen's sheds on the beach with the day's offerings posted on a blackboard.

Moot Hall, Aldeburgh

When it was first constructed around 1520, the lovely timber-framed Moot Hall stood in the centre of Aldeburgh, but over the years the sea has edged increasingly closer, giving the hall a prominent sea front location.

Thorpeness

A unique holiday village constructed in the early 1900s by the wealthy Scottish barrister, Glencairn Stuart Ogilvie, Thorpeness delights visitors with its mock Tudor and Jacobean architecture. Having bought up a sizeable plot of land, most of which was used for farming, Ogilvie created this fantasy for his own use, and invited family and friends to stay during the summer months. The village was still completely in the private ownership of the family up until the 1970s.

The Meare, Thorpeness

Thorpeness was laid out around a specially dug lake called The Meare. The focus of the village, the beautiful lake covers 64 acres and is themed around J.M. Barrie's famous children's book about Peter Pan and his friends, with little islands named after places in the story. Each August, the shallow lake plays host to the Thorpeness Regatta and fireworks display.

Thorpeness Beach

Before the fashionable resort of Thorpeness was created by a local landowner, it was a sleepy fishing hamlet called Thorpe. There is a steep shingle beach here with spectacular views towards Aldeburgh and along the Suffolk Heritage Coast, while the southern end of the beach forms the Haven Nature Reserve.

Thorpeness Windmill

Originally a corn mill at Aldringham two miles away, beautiful Thorpeness Windmill was built in 1824, but dismantled and moved to its present position in the early 1920s. The remarkable 'House in the Clouds', which greets visitors from its lofty heights, was originally the tank for the water used by the village.

Sizewell Beach

In an area once known for its bands of smugglers, Sizewell Beach still has a small fleet of fishing boats which draw up on the sandy beach near the little village. Part of the Suffolk Coast Path, the northern end is home to two nuclear power stations, while at the southern end stands Sizewell Hall which dates from the 1920s.

Leiston Abbey

The ruins of Leiston Abbey stand about two miles from the coast. Originally founded in 1183 at nearby Minsmere, it was rebuilt on its present site in 1363. A substantial amount remains including parts of the transepts, presbytery and lady chapel. Within the ruins there is a Georgian house which is now used for religious retreats.

Minsmere

Minsmere Nature Reserve is a haven for bird-watchers with numerous trails weaving through the 1,500 acres of marsh, heathland and woodland. These wetlands were created as part of the coastal defences during the Second World War and eventually bought by the RSPB in 1976. Some one hundred different species of birds breed here each year, amongst them avocet, bearded tit, bittern, marsh harrier and nightingale.

St. Peter's Church, Theberton

With its lovely thatched roof and delightful round tower, the interior of St. Peter's Church at Theberton is noted for its colourful geometric paintwork. Part of the framework of a German Zeppelin airship, which was shot down near here in 1917, is mounted in a glass case in the porch.

Westleton Heath

Another National Nature Reserve is found at Westleton Heath, which lies along the road to Dunwich. This important open heathland and light scrub is dominated by a variety of beautiful heathers which provide an important nectar source for native butterflies, including the rare Silver-studded Blue.

Dunwich Cliffs

The cliffs at Dunwich are of much geological interest and the constant erosion of this coastline has also claimed many buildings over the years. Scientists have located no fewer than six churches buried on the sea bed here. All Saints' Church reached the cliffs edge in 1904 and finally fell into the sea in 1922.

Dunwich Heath

Owned by The National Trust, Dunwich Heath and beach form an integral part of the Suffolk Coast and Heaths Area of Outstanding Natural Beauty. There are miles of wonderful walks over the heathland which was once part of the extensive Sandlings Heaths, and offshore seals and porpoises can be spotted playing in the sea.

Dingle Marshes, Dunwich

The peace and tranquility of the Dingle Marshes is in evidence as the sun rises and slowly burns off the morning mist. This RSPB Nature Reserve holds a mixture of freshwater and coastal habitats bordered by Dunwich Forest and the surrounding heathland. The marshes are controlled by grazing cattle in the summer.

Greyfriars

Once it was the seat of Saxon kings and a prosperous port, but today Dunwich consists of just a few cottages and a shingle beach. Numerous churches and houses now lie beneath the sea, and in 1739, the town centre finally collapsed leaving the ruins of the Franciscan friary of Greyfriars still standing.

Leper Hospital of St. James

The only remains of the leper colony hospital at Dunwich, the leper chapel stands in the grounds of the local parish church which was built much later in 1832. The hospital dates back to the 12th century when Dunwich was a flourishing port, and its chapel is one of only a handful of its kind left in the country.

Toby's Walks, Blythburgh

Near the village of Blythburgh are the delightful Toby's Walks, named after a member of the Suffolk Regiment, a Tobias Gill, who was hanged in 1750 for murdering a local servant girl on the common. Black Toby, as he was also known, was believed by many to have been innocently convicted and his ghost is said to still haunt this heathland. Despite its ghostly reputation, this is a beautiful spot for a walk or for having a picnic, and offers fine views of Blythburgh church.

Dunwich Forest

For many years, large parts of Dunwich Forest have consisted of managed conifer plantations, but plans are now in place to return the woodland to its original state of wilderness. The recent introduction of a flock of Dartmoor ponies is the first step in getting the forest back to its natural state, and over the next thirty to forty years, the pine trees here will be harvested and not replanted.

Walberswick

A footbridge across the River Blyth leads from Southwold to Walberswick, another attractive Suffolk village, situated on the southern shore of the estuary. At its heart, the pretty village green is bordered by some delightful cottages, little shops and traditional tearooms.

St. Andrew's Church, Walberswick
The Parish Church of St. Andrew is set within the dramatic ruins of a much grander 15th century church which fell into decay during the reign of Henry VIII. The smaller church, we see today, was built in the 1690s and holds memorials to fishermen lost at sea and an ancient consecrated stone slab used in medieval times by travelling priests.

Blythburgh Marshes

The large tidal lagoon of Blythburgh Water has been created over the years as the River Blyth burst through sea walls and land was now reclaimed from the sea. Surrounding it are endless marshes which are flooded at high tide and is a haven for wading birds at low tide. In a magnificent position at the edge of the marshes stands the impressive Holy Trinity Church, dwarfing the tiny village below.

Blythburgh

Once a thriving port, Blythburgh is now a peaceful little village lying on the River Blyth estuary, just inland from Southwold. Dominated by its magnificent church, the village has a number of interesting buildings and pretty cottages, such as these which stand in Priory Road near the remains of an Augustinian priory.

Holy Trinity Church, Blythburgh

The magnificent 15th century Holy Trinity Church at Blythburgh is known as the 'Cathedral of the Marshes'. Built on one of the earliest Christian sites in East Anglia, the roof of the impressive nave is adorned by medieval carved angels which were damaged by Cromwell's troops in 1644 who used them for target practice. From the top of the tower, there are panoramic views taking in the village and the tidal river with the wide open spaces of the surrounding marshland. During the Aldeburgh Festival, the church is also used a music venue as it has superb acoustics, a quality first discovered by Benjamin Britten in the 1960s.

Southwold

The charming seaside town of Southwold is considered the jewel in the crown of the Suffolk Heritage Coast. Although it is popular with visitors and holiday-makers, it remains a tranquil and unspoilt place. Almost built on an island, Southwold is enclosed to the north by Buss Creek and to the south by the River Blyth.

Southwold Lighthouse

In the centre of Southwold, surrounded by handsome Georgian townhouses, stands the fine white-walled lighthouse. It was completed in 1890 and replaced three older lighthouses which were under threat from coastal erosion at nearby Orford Ness. At its foot is the picturesque Sole Bay Inn, so named after a 1672 naval battle.

Southwold Harbour

Southwold's history as a fishing port goes back at least as far as the Domesday Book. The harbour, which is set at the mouth of the River Blyth a short way from the town centre, is always busy with pleasure craft and fishing boats. Here the banks are lined with boatyards and stalls where fresh fish and seafood are sold.

Southwold Pier

One of the finest piers in Britain, Southwold Pier underwent an extensive renovation programme from 1999 to 2001, one hundred years after it was first opened. It attracts many visitors, with its restaurants, shops and arcades and also has an active angling club whose members enjoy fishing off the end of the pier.

Walberswick Ferry
Today, a traditional rowing boat ferries pedestrians and cyclists across the River Blyth, connecting Walberswick and Southwold. A floating bridge chain ferry was first established here in 1885; later replaced by a steam ferry which ran until 1942 when changes to the harbour made the waters too rough to cross.

Hen Reedbeds, Reydon
Created as a nature reserve in the late 1990s to provide habitat for the bittern and other wildlife, the hen reedbeds at Reydon encompass reedbeds, fens, dykes and pools. Other wildlife include marsh harrier, heron, bearded tit, norfolk hawker and hobby, along with dragonflies and the secretive water vole and otters.

All Saints' Church, Frostenden

A small unassuming village on the road from Southwold to Lowestoft, Frostenden was registered in the Domesday Book as a small port with seagoing vessels tying up here. The village now lies three miles inland, and its name is said to mean means 'frogs' valley'. All Saints, with its round Saxon tower, lies adjacent to Frostenden Hall and is one of the oldest churches in Suffolk.

St. Andrew's Church, Covehithe

Within the crumbling shell of a much grander church stands the present Church of St. Andrew at Covehithe, four miles north of Southwold. The earlier church tower was incorporated when the new church was built in 1672, and it has been used as a landmark by sailors for hundreds of years. The small church is thatched, and inside, the original font has been preserved.

Kessingland

With views towards Lowestoft, charming Kessingland is another former fishing village on the Suffolk coast. It is today a popular holiday resort with a wide expanse of shingle beach, but also holds much archaeological importance as the remains of an ancient forest lie buried on the sea bed here.

Published in Great Britain by J. Salmon Ltd., Sevenoaks, Kent TN13 1BB.
Telephone 01732 452381 Email enquiries@jsalmon.co.uk
Design by John Curtis.
ISBN 978-1-84640-298-2
Printed in China.

Front cover photograph: Southwold Beach   Back cover photograph: Aldeburgh Beach
First Edition 2007   Revised Edition 2011